Conquering Grief Beyond Words

Her Daily Journal To Healing From Loss

May

Shanicka N. Scarbrough, MD

Printed in the United States of America
First Printing, 2018

ISBN-13: 978-1717040886
ISBN-10: 1717040888

Scriptures taken from the Holy Bible, English Standard Version®
(ESV) and Amplified Bible® (AMP)

DEDICATION

This journal is dedicated to the families of:
Stephon Clark
Trayvon Martin
Philando Castile
Jordan Davis
Sandra Bland
Michael Brown
Jordan Edwards
Eric Garner
Laquan McDonald
Tamir Rice
Dontre Hamilton
John Crawford III
Antonio Martin
Freddie Gray
...and the countless others who's shed blood have
rocked a nation to it's core.

The Lord is a stronghold for the oppressed,
a stronghold in times of trouble.
Psalm 9:9 (ESV)

ACKNOWLEDGEMENTS

It never ceases to amaze me how the Holy Spirit moves with each of these Her Daily Journals. As I was working on the 1st week, a song came on in my headphones that spoke to the core of what I was explaining in the story and I stopped in my tracks. Then it happened again while writing the second week, yet another song came on that caught my attention because of its portrayal of the words written on my pages. When it happened a 3rd time I just threw my hands up, smiled, and said, "Ok God, I got it!" This is how the soundtrack to our May journal, Conquering Grief Beyond Words was borne.

Just to give you another little tidbit on my process, God gives me the titles and subjects of these journals. If I come up with one on my own, He grieves my spirit and then drops something else that He had in mind instead. He even sends confirmations, some times through songs, people, signs that I see, etc. I'm so grateful that I am learning to trust and obey so that I can introduce to you a Savior who knows us intimately and wants to be a part of every decision we make.

Week 1
May 1st-7th

By His Stripes We are Healed...

We are sitting under the orange tree in the garden of my mother's home, surrounded by plush green grass and shrubbery, and I began to watch her as she slowly starts to doze off while she sits comfortably in her wheelchair, blue soft blanket with fluffy clouds and jolly sheep prancing through out its pattern wrapped loosely around her waist to her feet, with the intoxicating sweet smell of orange blossoms in the air. I inhale this aromatic fragrance and began to reflect on how peaceful and serene this moment is for the both of us.

This has not always been the case. In the early periods of my mother's progression through the various stages of Lewy Body Dementia, I would sit and just cry in total despair, totally disheartened by this diagnosis that even I as a physician could do nothing to bring about healing. I felt so helpless. I recall times when times like this I would lament as tears fell down my face, praying to God to change the diagnosis, mad and frustrated in the same moment at how "unfair this is" that my mother would be so young and lose all of her cognitive and motor functions. My mother's journey began in her late 40's and at the time of writing this journal she is 61 years old and is completely bed bound needing full assistance with her daily activities (eating, drinking, bathing, grooming, toileting, etc.)

I am very active in the care of my mother, so much so that at one point I wouldn't let anyone else take care of her but me. She became the center of my life when I moved to California, even though I was newly married, my mother was my 1st priority. I worked from home and attended to all of her needs, much to the detriment of my own health and sanity. I was beginning to dive, head 1st, back into an unrelenting depression that was threatening to burst to the surface. My husband, family and close friends were able to help me realize that I had made my mother an idol and had put God on the back burner of my life. An idol is simply something we reverence so much that we cannot focus on God.

The bible says that God is a jealous God and will not tolerate such idolatry. In the Old Testament we see idolatry plainly described as erected statues or items that were literally worshipped as gods. This is seen today as an idol can take the form of anything that you put before God, your health, a relationship, your career, etc. I fell deeply into that trap even though I had the best of intentions. Because of this, God got silent on me. I could not feel His presence (even though I know He was there) but I could not focus on His word.

It was not until I was able to fully release my mother to God, accepting that I have no say in the outcome of her life, I did not have the power to say whether she lived or died, only God has this control. Only God has all power in his hands. He sent His son Jesus Christ to be sacrificed for our benefit, including the healing of our bodies. Therefore, it is by the stripes Christ suffered at the hands of his accusers and the blood that was shed, that we are healed. But what exactly does that mean?

When Jesus walked this earth, he performed some amazing and often death-defying miracles, healing the sick from their infirmities, raising people from the dead and giving them a new lease on life. Today, God is still working those miracles in many people's lives. Many have been healed from cancers, HIV, or other disease, or have been delivered from accidents with injuries that should have killed them. We are all so quick to shout and thank God for saving us during those close calls!

But what happens when you or your loved one receives a poor prognosis and is given years, months, days or even hours to live. What if you lose a loved one from a battle with cancer or they were taken from you by the hands of a murderer? Are we still thankful? Are we still believing in God for a healing miracle? Are we still praising His name? Let me share with you why you should be.

When the bible teaches about healing, it is not just healing the physical body that is being spoken of. Jesus and his disciples performed many miracles because had they not, people would not believe that He was Lord with all power in his hands.

So Jesus said to him, "Unless you see signs and wonders you will not believe."
John 4:48 (ESV)

When you have accepted Christ as your personal Savior, then you are also promised eternal life or salvation. It is comforting to know that God has the power to heal on this side of heaven (earth) or the other. So while it is ok to be sad and upset when you receive that devastating news, do not stay in this place. It is ok to remember the good times and the life of the person that was taken or lament the suffering you are enduring or watching your loved one endure. But again, do not dwell in the depths of despair.

The key to conquering this grief is to truly put it on the alter and give it to God in prayer. Ask for God's peace beyond all understanding and that His will be done, regardless of the outcome. That is how I was able to find the peace and the strength to continue caring for my mother and not be consumed by what the situation looks like. I know that she had accepted Christ prior to her illness and I keep her covered in prayer. So I am at peace with whatever God's will is on her life, whether He heals her miraculously before my eyes, or if He will call her home and heal her in eternity. As Christians we must see past the natural and have faith in what God has already promised us, eternal life, where sickness and disease will be no more. Check out Hebrews 11:1 on faith. Tears and sorrow are only temporary, grab hold of God and let him carry those sorrows and burdens for you. He said His yolk is easy (Matthew 11:30). Just give your health and the health of your loved ones to the Lord and pray that His will be done and be at peace no matter what it looks like in the natural.

Inspirational Song Selection
The Hill - Travis Greene

My Prayer For You

Dear heavenly father, we come praising and blessing your name. Thank you for being the Great I Am. Thank you for sending your son, who endured suffering for our deliverance. We are grateful that we serve a God who knows our pain and is merciful. Thank you for every breath in our body, for every working cell and molecule. Lord, we pray that even if our health fails or we lose someone close to use to death, that you release your comfort and perfect peace over us so that we may endure until you call us home. We are thankful that you have already prepared a place for those who love you and obey your commandments. We know that to be absent from this body means we will be present with you. What a glorious revelation! Lord be a comfort for my sister who is grieving, who feels lost, who can't seem to find her way. Lord reveal healing powers to her so that in this time she draws nearer to you. It's in the mighty name of Jesus we pray. Amen!

May 1st

None of us lives for himself [for his own benefit, but for the Lord], and none of us dies for himself [but for the Lord]. If we live, we live for the Lord, and if we die, we die for the Lord. So then, whether we live or die, we are the Lord's. For Christ died and lived again for this reason, that He might be Lord of both the dead and the living.

Romans 14:7-9 (AMP)

Today's Prayer:

_____

_____

_____

_____

_____

_____

_____

_____

Self-Reflection:

_____

_____

_____

_____

_____

_____

_____

_____

Epiphany:

_____

_____

_____

_____

_____

_____

_____

_____

_____

_____

May 2nd

"Do not let your heart be troubled (afraid, cowardly). Believe [confidently] in God and trust in Him, [have faith, hold on to it, rely on it, keep going and] believe also in Me. In My Father's house are many dwelling places. If it were not so, I would have told you, because I am going there to prepare a place for you. And if I go and prepare a place for you, I will come back again and I will take you to Myself, so that where I am you may be also.

John 14:1-3 (AMP)

Today's Prayer:

_____

_____

_____

_____

_____

_____

Self-Reflection:

_____
_____
_____
_____
_____
_____
_____
_____

Epiphany:

_____
_____
_____
_____
_____
_____
_____
_____
_____

May 3rd

My flesh and my heart may fail, but God is the strength of my heart and my portion forever. For behold, those who are far from you shall perish; you put an end to everyone who is unfaithful to you. But for me it is good to be near God; I have made the Lord God my refuge, that I may tell of all your works.

Psalm 73:26-28 (ESV)

Today's Prayer:

_____

_____

_____

_____

_____

_____

_____

_____

13

Self-Reflection:

_____

_____

_____

_____

_____

_____

_____

_____

Epiphany:

_____

_____

_____

_____

_____

_____

_____

_____

_____

_____

May 4th

But [in fact] He has borne our griefs, And
He has carried our sorrows and pains; Yet
we [ignorantly] assumed that He was stricken,
Struck down by God and degraded and
humiliated [by Him]. But He was wounded
for our transgressions, He was crushed for
our wickedness [our sin, our injustice, our
wrongdoing]; The punishment [required] for
our well-being fell on Him, And by His stripes
(wounds) we are healed.
Isaiah 53:4-5 (AMP)

Today's Prayer:

_____

_____

_____

_____

_____

_____

_____

Self-Reflection:

_____

_____

_____

_____

_____

_____

_____

Epiphany:

_____

_____

_____

_____

_____

_____

_____

_____

_____

May 5th

Bless and affectionately praise the Lord,
O my soul,
And do not forget any of His benefits; Who
forgives all your sins, Who heals all your diseases;

Psalm 103:2-3 (AMP)

Today's Prayer:

_____

_____

_____

_____

_____

_____

_____

_____

_____

_____

_____

Self-Reflection:

_____

_____

_____

_____

_____

_____

_____

_____

Epiphany:

_____

_____

_____

_____

_____

_____

_____

_____

_____

_____

May 6th

And Jesus went throughout all the cities and villages, teaching in their synagogues and proclaiming the gospel of the kingdom and healing every disease and every affliction. When he saw the crowds, he had compassion for them, because they were harassed and helpless, like sheep without a shepherd.

1 Peter 5:8 (AMP)

Today's Prayer:

_____

_____

_____

_____

_____

_____

_____

_____

_____

_____

Self-Reflection:

_____
_____
_____
_____
_____
_____
_____
_____

Epiphany:

_____
_____
_____
_____
_____
_____
_____
_____
_____
_____

May 7th

Blessed be the God and Father of our Lord Jesus Christ! According to his great mercy, he has caused us to be born again to a living hope through the resurrection of Jesus Christ from the dead, to an inheritance that is imperishable, undefiled, and unfading, kept in heaven for you, who by God's power are being guarded through faith for a salvation ready to be revealed in the last time. In this you rejoice, though now for a little while, if necessary, you have been grieved by various trials, so that the tested genuineness of your faith—more precious than gold that perishes though it is tested by fire—may be found to result in praise and glory and honor at the revelation of Jesus Christ. Though you have not seen him, you love him. Though you do not now see him, you believe in him and rejoice with joy that is inexpressible and filled with glory, obtaining the outcome of your faith, the salvation of your souls.

1 Peter 1:3-9 (ESV)

Shanicka N. Scarbrough, MD

Today's Prayer:

_____

_____

_____

_____

_____

_____

_____

_____

_____

_____

_____

_____

_____

_____

_____

_____

_____

_____

_____

Self-Reflection:

_____

_____

_____

_____

_____

_____

_____

_____

Epiphany:

_____

_____

_____

_____

_____

_____

_____

_____

_____

Week 2
May 8th~14th

Relationship Status: It's Complicated

The pain and despair that follows a breakup can throw a person into a spiral of self-hate, self-depreciation, loathing of your ex, and a deep sadness that may feel like your heart is being ripped out of your chest, never to beat the same again. It doesn't matter whether this is your first relationship or puppy love or if you are unhappily married considering finality in divorce, the pain can be debilitating.

Break ups are hurtful, not only because of the lack of or fear of lack of companionship, but also because we have relinquished our hearts to this person, making ourselves susceptible and vulnerable to the scrutiny of our flaws. If our flaws are incompatible or unacceptable by our husbands or boyfriends, then we are open to internal reflection, questioning if we are worthy enough to be loved despite our short-comings. This vulnerability also sets us up to lash out at our partner, judging and pointing out their flaws, using these against them perpetuating the strife in the relationship. We find ourselves being quarrelsome and rigid, and we start this downward spiral of shaming, humiliating, disrespecting, and dishonoring our partners which could ultimately bring about the demise of the relationship. The opposite is true as well, as we may find ourselves to be on the receiving end of this spiral.

The pain of all of this could also lead individuals to do more than just endure the feelings of sadness. One may turn to alcohol or drugs, self-medicating to ease the pain. One might simply vow to never engage in a meaningful relationship again. Others may feel as though life is not worth living anymore and turn to thoughts of suicide or self mutilation. Yet another may become so bitter and angry that they are not able to maintain any other relationships because they are holding on to the pain from the previous relationship. It's such great news that we serve a God who can understand fully our suffering and has provided us with His comfort in our time of despair!

For just as Christ's sufferings are ours in abundance [as they overflow to His followers], so also our comfort [our reassurance, our encouragement, our consolation] is abundant through Christ [it is truly more than enough to endure what we must]. But if we are troubled and distressed, it is for your comfort and salvation; or if we are comforted and encouraged, it is for your comfort, which works [in you] when you patiently endure the same sufferings which we experience. And our hope for you [our confident expectation of good for you] is firmly grounded [assured and unshaken], since we know that just as you share as partners in our sufferings, so also you share as partners in our comfort.
1 Corinthians 1:5-7 (AMP)

Is that not the most amazing thing ever?!? It brings me so much joy knowing that God does not want me to suffer, but if I do, He is right there to give me the ultimate love, support, and comfort from a Father to a daughter. The weight can be lifted is we only come to Him during our desperation and give us unspeakable joy even in the midst of our pain.

God's unconditional love negates all of our imperfections, and he is forgiving and accepting of us for who we are in Him (his imperfect creations) even if the object of our affection does not. God admonishes us to love one another (as a neighbor, coworker, family member, person living on the street, your boss, and yes even your ex!) as He loves us and His church. Although you may be in pain now, take heed to forgive and love (even if from a distance) your ex as it is in line with being obedient to God and his commandments. His desire is for us to live harmoniously with one another in Christ. Take a look and Romans 15:5-6 and then the verse below.

"I am giving you a new commandment, that you love one another. Just as I have loved you, so you too are to love one another. By this everyone will know that you are My disciples, if you have love *and* unselfish concern for one another."
John 13:34-35 (AMP)

As you strive to be more like Christ, the more difficult carnal, worldly relationships will be for you. Those "friends with benefit" and late night "booty calls" you will become less tolerant of, finding yourself desiring deeper and more meaningful interactions with your love interest. It is vital that during your time of dating, leading up to marriage (if that is God's will on your life), that you seek God 1st, requesting knowledge of His will, wisdom, and discernment in your romantic relationships. So when your morals begin to not line up with your partner's, it's ok to have that potentially heartbreaking conversation of leaving, but know that you will not remain in this broken state and season because of God's love and compassion for you.

God wants you to be connected with a partner who is striving to be more like Him, who seeks His face earnestly, just as you are (2 Corinthians 6:14), honoring Him through your time spent together. When this doesn't line up, neither does the relationship, no matter how good he smells, how kindly he treats you, the money he spends on you, or how good he is in bed. May women stay in those relationships because of those external things which truly hold no weight in the determination of a Godly relationship.

The pain you feel during this difficult time of breakup is but only temporary (Psalm 30:5) and the only way to come out of this pain unscathed without carrying baggage to the next relationship (meaning lingering depression, self-loathing, unforgiveness, etc.) is to truly put all of your trust in our creator who wants you to live an abundant life according to His will. In your walk with Christ, you have to learn to hear God's voice through the Holy Spirit, and the more you are able to hear Him, the more you are able to actually obey what He asks of you. If that means to be still, then be obedient in doing so.

It is also important to note that our trials (including but not limited to the dissolution of a relationship) are not designed to break us, but to shape and mold you into who God wants you to be. Trials are the testing of our faith. God did not promise us that we would be without sorrow and pain, but thankfully He did promise us perfect peace through Him in the midst of our difficult times if we leave our cares and troubles with Him. Our trials, sorrows and pain help refine us and should increase our faith in knowing that God's got it!

Repenting plays a huge role in our relationship with Christ. Ask God to reveal to you the sins you committed while in this relationship so that you can acknowledge them AND ask for forgiveness. You are saved by Jesus's blood as he became sin for us while dying on the cross so that we might be forgiven. This simple act is like a healing balm to your soul and helps you to move forward past the hurt.

Our God is gracious and loving God and, despite what you may think while you are going through the pain, He wants you to have companionship (Genesis 2:18) and a healthy relationship. It is vital that you also be at peace in whatever season you are in, (single, married, courting, divorced, etc.) continuing to honor Him above any of the circumstances you find yourself in. Be content in God's will for your life and body (His temple) even if it does not involve you having a partner to spend the rest of your life with. Your praise and God's grace and mercy is sufficient to heal your broken heart and spirit.

Inspirational Song Selection:

Live Through It - James Fortune & FIYA

My Prayer for You:

Blessed Father, God almighty, we give all of our praises to you! We just want to take this time to thank you for being who you are, loving us the way that you do, even when it feels like we are not worthy to be loved by anyone. I pray right now for my sister who is hurting, going from relationship to relationship, becoming discouraged at her being able to find true love. Lord, show her through your loving grace what unconditional love really means. Show her how to honor you by honoring her life, her body, and her mind, prayerfully staying focused on you. Help her hear your voice so that she may be able to discern who you have for her. Heal her broken heart from past hurts. Lord, reveal to her her own sins that she may have committed during these relationships so that she may repent and receive your forgiveness. Help her to forgive herself and the ones who hurt her as well. We bless you in this moment and always. Its in the mighty name of Jesus. Amen!

May 8th

Do not be unequally bound together with unbelievers [do not make mismatched alliances with them, inconsistent with your faith]. For what partnership can righteousness have with lawlessness? Or what fellowship can light have with darkness? What harmony can there be between Christ and Belial (Satan)? Or what does a believer have in common with an unbeliever? What agreement is there between the temple of God and idols? For we are the temple of the living God;

2 Corinthians 6:14-16 (AMP)

Today's Prayer:

_____

_____

_____

_____

_____

Self-Reflection:

_____
_____
_____
_____
_____
_____
_____

Epiphany:

_____
_____
_____
_____
_____
_____
_____
_____
_____

May 9th

For this is the will of God, that you be sanctified [separated and set apart from sin]: that you abstain and back away from sexual immorality; that each of you know how to control his own body in holiness and honor [being available for God's purpose and separated from things profane], not [to be used] in lustful passion, like the Gentiles who do not know God and are ignorant of His will;

1 Thessalonians 4:3-5 (AMP)

Today's Prayer:

_____

_____

_____

_____

_____

_____

_____

Self-Reflection:

_____

_____

_____

_____

_____

_____

_____

_____

Epiphany:

_____

_____

_____

_____

_____

_____

_____

_____

_____

May 10th

Hide your face from my sins, and
blot out all my iniquities.
Create in me a clean heart, O God, and renew a
right spirit within me. Cast me not away from your
presence, and take not your Holy Spirit from
me. Restore to me the joy of your salvation, and
uphold me with a willing spirit.

Psalm 51:9-12 (ESV)

Today's Prayer:

_____

_____

_____

_____

_____

_____

_____

_____

Self-Reflection:

_____

_____

_____

_____

_____

_____

_____

Epiphany:

_____

_____

_____

_____

_____

_____

_____

_____

May 11th

He heals the brokenhearted and binds up their wounds. He determines the number of the stars; he gives to all of them their names. Great is our Lord, and abundant in power; his understanding is beyond measure.

Psalm 147:3-5 (ESV)

Today's Prayer:

_____

_____

_____

_____

_____

_____

_____

_____

_____

_____

_____

Self-Reflection:

_____

_____

_____

_____

_____

_____

_____

_____

Epiphany:

_____

_____

_____

_____

_____

_____

_____

_____

_____

May 12th

His delight is not in the strength of the horse,
nor his pleasure in the legs of a man, but the Lord
takes pleasure in those who fear him, in those who
hope in his steadfast love.
Psalm 147:10-11

Today's Prayer:

_____

_____

_____

_____

_____

_____

_____

_____

_____

_____

_____

_____

Self-Reflection:

_____
_____
_____
_____
_____
_____
_____
_____

Epiphany:

_____
_____
_____
_____
_____
_____
_____
_____
_____
_____

May 13th

Out of the depths I cry to you, O Lord! O Lord, hear my voice! Let your ears be attentive to the voice of my pleas for mercy! If you, O Lord, should mark iniquities, O Lord, who could stand? But with you there is forgiveness, that you may be feared. I wait for the Lord, my soul waits, and in his word I hope; my soul waits for the Lord more than watchmen for the morning, more than watchmen for the morning.

Psalm 130:1-6 (ESV)

Today's Prayer:

_____

_____

_____

_____

_____

_____

_____

Self-Reflection:

_____
_____
_____
_____
_____
_____
_____
_____

Epiphany:

_____
_____
_____
_____
_____
_____
_____
_____
_____
_____

May 14th

Sing to the Lord, O you His godly ones, And give thanks at the mention of His holy name. For His anger is but for a moment, His favor is for a lifetime. Weeping may endure for a night, But a shout of joy comes in the morning.

Psalm 30:4-5 (AMP)

Today's Prayer:

_____

_____

_____

_____

_____

_____

_____

_____

_____

_____

_____

Self-Reflection:

_____
_____
_____
_____
_____
_____
_____
_____

Epiphany:

_____
_____
_____
_____
_____
_____
_____
_____
_____
_____
_____

Week 3
May 15th-21st

Cash Rules Everything Around Me

We live in a capitalistic world with a clear socioeconomic division between the "Haves" and the "Have Nots." Everything society portrays via social media, big and small screens, as well as in the music we listen to glorifies a way of life some people would do just about anything to obtain. It's evident in each individual's daily grind with the ultimate goal of increasing financial wealth and security, creating a life that is comfortable and filled with the things that only money can buy. One's status in society is determined by your net worth, how much you own minus how much you owe. Based on this simple calculation, that number could either be a positive or negative and the more you are in the black the higher you climb on the social latter of what those around us deems as success.

We, as a society, have become obsessed with how much we can accumulate and the keeping up of appearances of having more than we actually have. In this realm it is very easy to do one of two things:

1. Thank God for all of your fortune, favor and/or fame.
2. Delude yourself into thinking that you have accomplished this all on your own.

When times are well it is easy to give God praise and be thankful. We may even, in our own vanity, forget to humble ourselves and in error believe that our accomplishments were all our own doing through hard work and dedication to the hustle and grind. Just take a moment and reflect on the time when you felt like all was right in world. You were looking and smelling good, hair fried, dyed and laid to the side, your shoe game was on point, your car was glistening in the sunlight, all of your bills were paid, you had a little change in your pocket and even in the bank, nails and pedicure on fleek. I can almost guarantee you were not laid out prostrate in front of God in reverence for Him being the provider that He is, has been and always will be. If you were, then YAAASSS QUEEN, YOU GET IT!

What happens when all seems completely loss with no foreseeable way out. What is your state of mind and spirit when your bank account becomes depleted and is in the red and you are now struggling to figure out how you will pay that bill with the red glowing stamp indicating that it is past due. The house is in foreclosure, they have repossessed your car, the eviction notice is plastered to your door, the kids are crying because their little bellies are hungry and you have no idea where your next meal is going to come from. Is this the time you lay prostate before Him?

Any or all of these scenarios are enough to send you tumbling head first into the depths of despair. Especially in a society that celebrates when you are on top but shuns you during the most difficult times of your life when you seemingly have nothing. You find yourself alone and in a state of panic, frustration, embarrassment and confusion. You begin to grieve for everything that you have lost or have been longing for what you think you are entitled to. You can respond to this one of 3 ways:

1. Shut out the world and succumb to the numbing depression, disconnecting from reality and begin "self medicating" (i.e. alcohol, drugs, or other addictive behaviors, or even suicide).

2. Allow your current situation to be a catalyst to "pull yourself up by your bootstraps", motivating you to do whatever is necessary to "get this money", regardless of the potential negative consequences (i.e. lie, steal, cheat, hurt, and kill).

3. Lay your troubles on the altar, listen for God's guidance and instruction, and be obedient to His will, trusting and activating your faith, giving praise to Him all the while.

Let me assure you, NONE of these choices are easy, but I will submit to you reasons why #3 is the best choice regardless of what your situation looks like.

Consider Job, a very wealthy and well respected man whom God highly favored with wealth, a large family, extensive flock and servants. Job loved and feared God so much that he was very careful to keep His life pure before Him. Job was such the apple of God's eye that He bragged to Satan about him. Satan argued that Job was only loyal to God because He had given Job such a lavishly favored life. Therefore, he petitioned to God to allow him afflict Job in an effort to prove that

Job would surely curse God when times were bad. God gave Satan the go ahead as long as he didn't touch a hair on Job's head.

Being the slickster that Satan is, he goes on to completely wipe out Job's offspring (all of his son's and his son's wives), his livestock, and his servants (except for 2 witnesses) and he did this all in one day! Can you imagine losing the lives of your children and all of your wealth and help in the course of minutes of each other! Talk about a devastatingly catastrophic day! Job's world had been completely turned upside down, and to top it all off, God sanctioned it!

Now Job was in utter despair and he immediately began tearing at his own clothes, crying out in so much pain, mourning the loss of his children. But Job did something else in that instance, something that may surprise most. He fell down to his knees and he WORSHIPED GOD.

He said, "Naked (without possessions) I came [into this world] from my mother's womb, And naked I will return there. The Lord gave and the Lord has taken away;

<u>Blessed be the name of the Lord</u>."

Through all this Job did not sin nor did he blame God.

Job 1:21-22 (AMP)

Much to Satan's surprise, Job still maintained his loyalty to God, even though he was experience extreme circumstances and tragedy.

Of course, Satan is mad as H-E-Double Hockey Sticks as God begins to rightfully brag on his son Job for still giving Him praise even in the midst of his sorrow. Satan petitions God again, and the confident and all knowing master grants him his wish, this time with the stipulation that Satan cannot take Job's life.

Satan then throws everything he's got at Job, afflicting him with painful boils and sores from the top of his head to the bottom of his feet. Job became so sick that even his wife told him to "curse God and die!" Job chastised his wife saying that she was acting like those who were spiritually ignorant of God's will. He said,

"Shall we indeed accept [only] good from God

and not [also] accept adversity *and* disaster?"

Job 2:10 (AMP).

Job refuses to curse God. But this does not mean that he was not hurting. Job fell into such a deep depression that he spends an entire chapter (Job 3) lamenting on how horrible his life was and he wished that he was never born. His own friends tried to convince him that he must have done something egregious to deserve what had come upon him. They also said that his son's must have done something terrible and that they were getting what they deserved. To add salt to insult, his friends even told him that he probably should have been "punished" even more than he was for whatever he had done to deserve this wrath from God and to ask God for forgiveness and seek His favor. (Job 4-15)

Job becomes very irritated with his "so called friends" whose intent seems only to tear him down during his time of sorrow. Job admits that he cannot understand God's ways or fathom why he would allow those who are good to suffer while those who are evil seem to undergo no hardships. Job cannot fathom the reasons for his suffering, but he is clear that his God is sovereign, is a redeemer, and that he has a blameless record in heaven.(Job 16:18; Job 19:25). Job goes back and forth with his friends, staying firm in the belief that God will see him through. Even though Job had questions for God, his reverence did not falter.

"As God lives, who has taken away my right *and* denied me justice, And the Almighty, who has cause bitterness *and* grief for my soul, As long as my life is within me, And the breath of God is [still] in my nostrils, My lips will not speak unjustly. Nor will my tongue utter deceit. "Far be it from me that I should admit you are right [in your accusations against me]; Until I die, I will not remove my integrity from me. "I hold fast my uprightness *and* my right standing with God and I will not let them go; My heart does not reproach me for any of my days.
Job 27:2-6 (AMP)

God, growing tired of this banter, interrupts

Job and his friends, irritated that they questioned His authority, wisdom and unequivocal power. He poses a series of questions demonstrating just how much power God has in his hands. Job humbles himself, acknowledging that he knows nothing of God's infinite wisdom and repents.

God turns HIs wrath to Job's friends because they spoke untruths about God and requires that they provide a sacrifice. He also states that He will only accept the prayers of Job to intercede on their behalf so that God would not punish them to the extent that they truly deserve.

After Job prayed for those who sought to harm him with words while grieving, God restored Job's wealth 2 fold! God gave him twice the fortune, more livestock and servants than he had before, 10 more children and after this lived another 140 years! Talk about restoration!

Although Job spent a significant time in despair, questioning the fairness of God, when he repented of his sins against God and even praying for his "friends", God honored his faith. The lesson here is clear. God did not promise us as Christians that we are not going to suffer.

When you come across financial gains as well as financial hardships, put your trust in the God who wants you to have victory in Him. Trust that He will see you through. Now is not the time to give, now is the time to PRAY up!

Inspirational Song Selection:

Come as You Are - Snoop Dogg; featuring Marvin Sapp and Mary Mary

My Prayer for You:

Blessed is the name of Jesus! We glorify and exalt your name. We come to you with bowed heads and uplifted hearts to thank you for being a God who sent a Son who can relate to our suffering. We know that it is not your desire for your children to hurt and thank God you provided us a way out of misery by simply trusting and obeying you! Our suffering bares obedience to your will. Let your will be done! Gracious father, I pray that my sister becomes or maintains good stewardship over her finances, making sound financial decisions with the help of the Holy Spirit. I pray that, regardless of wealth or if she ever falls in the pits of despair because of financial or material loss, I pray that she remains focused on you and you draw her closer to you.

May 15th

And we know that for those who love God all things work together for good, for those who are called according to his purpose.

Romans 8:28 (ESV)

Today's Prayer:

_____

_____

_____

_____

_____

_____

_____

_____

_____

_____

_____

_____

_____

Self-Reflection:

_____
_____
_____
_____
_____
_____
_____

Epiphany:

_____
_____
_____
_____
_____
_____
_____
_____

May 16th

And calling the crowd to him with his disciples, he said to them, "If anyone would come after me, let him deny himself and take up his cross and follow me. For whoever would save his life will lose it, but whoever loses his life for my sake and the gospel's will save it. For what does it profit a man to gain the whole world and forfeit his soul? For what can a man give in return for his soul? For whoever is ashamed of me and of my words in this adulterous and sinful generation, of him will the Son of Man also be ashamed when he comes in the glory of his Father with the holy angels."

Mark 8:34–38 (ESV)

Today's Prayer:

_____

_____

_____

_____

_____

_____

Self-Reflection:

_____

_____

_____

_____

_____

_____

_____

_____

Epiphany:

_____

_____

_____

_____

_____

_____

_____

_____

_____

_____

May 17th

For promotion cometh neither from the east, nor from the west, nor from the south. But God is the judge: he putteth down one, and setteth up another.

Psalm 75:6-7 (KJV)

Today's Prayer:

_____

_____

_____

_____

_____

_____

_____

_____

_____

_____

_____

Self-Reflection:

_____

_____

_____

_____

_____

_____

_____

_____

Epiphany:

_____

_____

_____

_____

_____

_____

_____

_____

_____

May 18th

Be still before the Lord and wait patiently for him; fret not yourself over the one who prospers in his way, over the man who carries out evil devices! Refrain from anger, and forsake wrath! Fret not yourself; it tends only to evil. For the evildoers shall be cut off, but those who wait for the Lord shall inherit the land.

Psalm 37:7-9 (ESV)

Today's Prayer:

_____

_____

_____

_____

_____

_____

_____

_____

_____

Self-Reflection:

_____

_____

_____

_____

_____

_____

_____

Epiphany:

_____

_____

_____

_____

_____

_____

_____

_____

_____

May 19th

Bring all the tithes (the tenth) into the storehouse, so that there may be food in My house, and test Me now in this," says the Lord of hosts, "if I will not open for you the windows of heaven and pour out for you [so great] a blessing until there is no more room to receive it.

Malachi 3:10 (AMP)

Today's Prayer:

_____

_____

_____

_____

_____

_____

_____

_____

_____

_____

Self-Reflection:

_____

_____

_____

_____

_____

_____

_____

_____

Epiphany:

_____

_____

_____

_____

_____

_____

_____

_____

_____

May 20th

Behold, here is what I have seen to be good and fitting: to eat and drink, and to find enjoyment in all the labor in which he labors under the sun during the few days of his life which God gives him—for this is his [allotted] reward. Also, every man to whom God has given riches and possessions, He has also given the power and ability to enjoy them and to receive [this as] his [allotted] portion and to rejoice in his labor—this is the gift of God [to him]. For he will not often consider the [troubled] days of his life, because God keeps him occupied and focused on the joy of his heart [and the tranquility of God indwells him].

Ecclesiastes 5:18-20 (AMP)

Today's Prayer:

_____

_____

_____

_____

_____

Self-Reflection:

_____

_____

_____

_____

_____

_____

_____

Epiphany:

_____

_____

_____

_____

_____

_____

_____

_____

May 21st

"No one can serve two masters; for either he will hate the one and love the other, or he will be devoted to the one and despise the other. You cannot serve God and mammon [money, possessions, fame, status, or whatever is valued more than the Lord].

Matthew 6:24 (AMP)

Today's Prayer:

_____

_____

_____

_____

_____

_____

_____

_____

_____

_____

Self~Reflection:

_____

_____

_____

_____

_____

_____

_____

Epiphany:

_____

_____

_____

_____

_____

_____

_____

Weeks 4~5
May 22nd~31st

Beauty for Ashes

We all will return to the dust someday. Hearing these words are not very comforting, especially when we are made aware of our mortality. We may wish to live forever, but that is not our reality. Death is a part of each of our lives. No one is exempt. You can't buy, beg, or plead your way out of this truth.

The pain you feel as a result of the death of a loved one is oftentimes overwhelming, especially if the death was unexpected. It is one thing know it's coming, for example, the loss of a loved one to a long battle with cancer, but a totally different experience if your loved one died suddenly and unexpectedly, like in a car crash or the victim of senseless violence. In either scenario (expected or unexpected) you never really feel completely prepared for the agony that is to come with the loss.

Jesus was not impervious to our suffering when it comes to the ramifications of death of a loved one on the survivor. When Martha had gotten word to Jesus to tell him his friend and her brother, Lazarus had fallen ill, Jesus already knew that Lazarus was going to die. After hearing this, Jesus said,

"This illness does not lead to death. It is for the glory of God, so that the Son of God may be glorified through it."

John 11:4 (ESV)

If only in our present day we could take comfort knowing these words Jesus spoke millennia ago! Let's dig a little deeper into what that actually means for you.

After Jesus received this bad news, he did not leave right away. He stayed where he was for two more days when Lazarus died. Jesus didn't need anyone else to bring the news that Lazarus had died because he already knew and began preparing him and his disciples to travel. By the time Jesus made his way to Judea, Lazarus had been in the tomb for 4 days.

Martha meets Jesus on the road, crying out that if only Jesus had come sooner, her brother would not have died. Jesus let's her know that Lazarus will be resurrected from his grave.

Jesus said to her, "I am the resurrection and the life. Whoever believes in me, though he die, yet shall he live, and everyone who lives and believes in me shall never die. Do you believe this?"

John 11:25-26

This is the good news that we should focus on when we encounter the sting of death. We are reassured by our heavenly Father that we will be resurrected and take our place in heaven with Him and live eternally. Criteria? Believe in Christ.

Martha then turns and summons her sister Mary who gets up quickly to run to her Savior, with her friends and family (Jews in the scripture whom actually wanted Jesus dead) who were consoling her during her mourning following close behind her. When she encounters God, she sorrowfully cries as she falls at his feet that her brother could've been saved had Jesus only been there sooner. When Jesus sees Mary and the Jews that had accompanied her weeping , he was deeply moved, so much so that he himself began to cry (John 11:35).

This short two word scripture, "Jesus wept", is such an impactful one in that it gives us a clear picture of the nature of our Savior. Although Jesus had the power to keep Lazarus from dying, he allowed it so that God could get the most glory out of the situation. Even though Jesus allowed this to happen, he was greatly affected by it emotionally because of the suffering the family and those who loved Lazarus had to endure. You can rest in the fact that God does not take pleasure in our pain. He knows our moans and groans but He promises that the grief is only for but a season.

Jesus was then taken to the tomb where Lazarus had been dead for 4 days. Jesus was still weeping when he told them to roll back the stone that was in place in the doorway of the tomb. Jesus lifted up his eyes to heaven, prayed to the Father out loud (only so that the spectators could believe), then called out in a loud voice, "Lazarus, come out!" (John 11:43) With that, Lazarus arose from the dead!

You may not understand God's ways, no finite mind can so you are in good company! But you do have a choice in believing that God can do the miraculous and snatch someone from the claws of death to show those watching that He is able to do it or He can allow the suffering and pain with a bigger picture in mind that would bring others to Christ who would otherwise never have had an encounter with God. Only our Father knows the date and time we will take our last breath. But even in our death, God will get the glory. Be comforted in knowing that no matter what the situation looks like, He is in control. All that He asks of you is to trust His will, even if you don't understand it, and stand firm in the knowledge of your eternal salvation, a gift that only God can bestow once you believe and faithfully stand on His word.

Inspirational song selections:

1. Trust in You - Anthony Brown & group therAPy
2. Whoa! - Bryan Andrew Wilson

My Prayer for You:

Heavenly Father, thank you for being a God who knows how to comfort us in our time of need. Thank you for sacrificing your son for our good. Lord we ask you to wipe our tears and bring us peace of mind when we are confronted by the death of a loved one. We rejoice in knowing that if we believe in Christ, that you will grant us eternal life with you. We pray for all of our family and friends, interceding on their behalf that they come to have a personal relationship with you. We understand that we have no control over their salvation, but we ask that you begin to draw them closer to you so that on their death beds they can be assured to receive the same eternal life that you promised us. Thank you Lord for your compassion, grace and mercy. It's in the mighty name of Jesus we pray, amen!

May 22nd

This is my comfort in my affliction,
that your promise gives me life.

Psalm 119:50 (ESV)

Today's Prayer:

_____

_____

_____

_____

_____

_____

_____

_____

_____

_____

_____

_____

_____

_____

Self-Reflection:

_____
_____
_____
_____
_____
_____
_____

Epiphany:

_____
_____
_____
_____
_____
_____
_____
_____
_____

May 23rd

For if He causes grief, Then He will have
compassion
According to His abundant lovingkindness and
tender mercy. For He does not afflict willingly
and from His heart
Or grieve the children of men.

Lamentations 3:32-33 (AMP)

Today's Prayer:

_____

_____

_____

_____

_____

_____

_____

_____

_____

_____

Self~Reflection:

_____

_____

_____

_____

_____

_____

_____

_____

Epiphany:

_____

_____

_____

_____

_____

_____

_____

_____

_____

May 24th

"Do not let your heart be troubled (afraid, cowardly). Believe [confidently] in God and trust in Him, [have faith, hold on to it, rely on it, keep going and] believe also in Me. In My Father's house are many dwelling places. If it were not so, I would have told you, because I am going there to prepare a place for you. And if I go and prepare a place for you, I will come back again and I will take you to Myself, so that where I am you may be also"

John 14:1-3 (AMP)

Today's Prayer:

_____

_____

_____

_____

_____

_____

Self-Reflection:

_____

_____

_____

_____

_____

_____

_____

_____

Epiphany:

_____

_____

_____

_____

_____

_____

_____

_____

_____

May 25th

"I will not leave you as orphans [comfortless, bereaved, and helpless]; I will come [back] to you. After a little while the world will no longer see Me, but you will see Me; because I live, you will live also."

John 14:18-19 (AMP)

Today's Prayer:

_____

_____

_____

_____

_____

_____

_____

_____

_____

_____

_____

Self-Reflection:

_____

_____

_____

_____

_____

_____

_____

_____

Epiphany:

_____

_____

_____

_____

_____

_____

_____

_____

_____

_____

_____

May 26th

Peace I leave with you; My [perfect] peace I give to you; not as the world gives do I give to you. Do not let your heart be troubled, nor let it be afraid. [Let My perfect peace calm you in every circumstance and give you courage and strength for every challenge.] You heard Me tell you, 'I am going away, and I am coming back to you.' If you [really] loved Me, you would have rejoiced, because I am going [back] to the Father, for the Father is greater than I.

John 14:27-28 (ESV)

Today's Prayer:

_____

_____

_____

_____

_____

_____

Self-Reflection:

_____

_____

_____

_____

_____

_____

_____

_____

Epiphany:

_____

_____

_____

_____

_____

_____

_____

_____

_____

May 27th

For we know that if the earthly tent [our physical body] which is our house is torn down [through death], we have a building from God, a house not made with hands, eternal in the heavens.

2 Corinthians 5:1-2 (AMP)

Today's Prayer:

_____

_____

_____

_____

_____

_____

_____

_____

_____

_____

_____

Self-Reflection:

_____

_____

_____

_____

_____

_____

_____

_____

Epiphany:

_____

_____

_____

_____

_____

_____

_____

_____

_____

May 28th

For we walk by faith, not by sight [living our lives in a manner consistent with our confident belief in God's promises] we are [as I was saying] of good courage and confident hope, and prefer rather to be absent from the body and to be at home with the Lord. Therefore, whether we are at home [on earth] or away from home [and with Him], it is our [constant] ambition to be pleasing to Him.

2 Corinthians 5:7-9 (AMP)

Today's Prayer:

_____

_____

_____

_____

_____

_____

_____

_____

Self-Reflection:

_____

_____

_____

_____

_____

_____

_____

_____

Epiphany:

_____

_____

_____

_____

_____

_____

_____

_____

_____

May 29th

You have turned for me my mourning into dancing;
you have loosed my sackcloth and
clothed me with gladness,
that my glory may sing your praise and not be
silent. O Lord my God, I will give thanks to you
forever!

Psalm 30:11-12 (ESV)

Today's Prayer:

_____

_____

_____

_____

_____

_____

_____

_____

_____

_____

_____

Self-Reflection:

_____
_____
_____
_____
_____
_____
_____

Epiphany:

_____
_____
_____
_____
_____
_____
_____
_____
_____

Self-Reflection:

_____

_____

_____

_____

_____

_____

_____

_____

Epiphany:

_____

_____

_____

_____

_____

_____

_____

_____

_____

_____

May 30th

For godly grief produces a repentance that leads to salvation without regret, whereas worldly grief produces death.

2 Corinthians 7:10 (ESV)

Today's Prayer:

_____

_____

_____

_____

_____

_____

_____

_____

_____

_____

_____

_____

_____

Self-Reflection:

Epiphany:

May 31st

He will wipe away every tear from their eyes, and death shall be no more, neither shall there be mourning, nor crying, nor pain anymore, for the former things have passed away.

Revelation 21:4 (ESV)

Today's Prayer:

_____

_____

_____

_____

_____

_____

_____

_____

_____

_____

_____

_____

Self-Reflection:

_____
_____
_____
_____
_____
_____
_____
_____

Epiphany:

_____
_____
_____
_____
_____
_____
_____
_____
_____
_____

ABOUT THE AUTHOR

Dr. Shanicka N. Scarbrough (aka America's Favorite Family Doctor) graduated from the University of Illinois College of Medicine in 2009 and completed her family medicine residency program at Advocate Christ Medical Center in 2012. Since then, she has gained invaluable experience as a board-certified family medicine physician and has had the privilege of owning and operating a private medical practice. She now teaches other physicians and physicians-in-training how to start their own medical practice with her bestselling book, The Lunchtime Physician Entrepreneur, and her live virtual courses in the Road to Private Practice Academy.

Having hosted the The DivaMD radio show on Urban Broadcast Media, and continuing to contribute to a variety of other platforms on television and social media, she speaks in various educational settings and travels internationally, including to Haiti, Liberia, and Cape Town South Africa, to extend her knowledge, skills, and expertise across the globe.

Dr. Shanicka has also released her 1st anthology and bestselling book, As the Wind Blows, a collection of seven women's stories of weakness, including her own, and how they overcame life's obstacles. Dr. Shanicka's mission is to be transparent about her life in hopes that sharing her testimonies will help bring others closer to God.

The Her Daily Journal Monthly Series was a God-given vision to release one interactive journal a month with a new topic to foster a deeper understanding of self and increase the reader's relationship with Christ by providing biblical application to every day life. Be on the look out for the June journaling experience!

To connect, visit her website at
www.DrShanicka.com

To subscribe each month, go to
bit.ly/HerDailyJournalSubscribe

Made in the USA
Lexington, KY
05 May 2018